ENCOURAGEMENT CAFE DEVOTIONAL COLORING JOURNAL
VOLUME II

Copyright © Encouragement Café Ministries, Inc., 2018
All Rights Reserved.

Cover design by Betty 'B' Shoopman featuring Lisa Albinus' art.
Inside Illustrations by Lisa Albinus, Noelle Okolowicz, Betty 'B' Shoopman,
Hannah-Rose Albinus, Grace Ann Mills, and Luann Prater

Published by Betty 'B' Shoopman | B New Creations, Gulf Breeze, FL 32563
ISBN 978-0-9984648-4-8

No portion of this book may be reproduced, stored in a retrieval system, or transmitted in any form or by any means - electronic, mechanical, photocopy, recording, scanning, or any other - except for brief quotations in critical reviews or articles, without the prior written permission of Encouragement Café Ministries, Inc.

Scripture quotations marked (NIV) are from The Holy Bible, New International Version®, NIV®. Copyright© 1973, 1978, 1984, 2011 by Biblica, Inc.™ Used by permission of Zondervan. All rights reserved worldwide.www.zondervan.com The "New International Version" and "NIV" are registered trademarks of Biblica, Inc.™ Used with permission.

Scripture quotations marked (NASB) are from The New American Standard Bible (NASB)®, Copyright© 1960, 1962, 1963, 1968, 1971, 1972, 1973,1975, 1977, 1995 by The Lockman Foundation Used by permission.

Scripture quotations marked (ESV) are from The Holy Bible, English Standard Version® (ESV®), Copyright © 2001 by Crossway, a publishing ministry of Good News Publishers. Used by permission. All rights reserved. The "ESV" and "English Standard Version" are trademarks of Good News Publishers. Used with permission.

Scripture quotations marked (KJV) are from the New King James Version®. Copyright© 1982 by Thomas Nelson, Inc. Used by permission. All rights reserved.

Scripture quotations marked (MSG) are from The Message. Copyright©1993, 1994, 1995, 1996, 2000, 2001, 2002. Used by permission of NavPress Publishing Group.

Scripture quotations marked (NLT) are from the Holy Bible, New Living Translation, Copyright 1996, 2004, 2007 by Tyndale House Foundation. Used by permission of Tyndale House Publishers, Inc., Carol Stream, Illinois 60188. All rights reserved.

Scripture quotations marked (HCSB) are from the Holman Christian Standard Bible®, Copyright© 1999, 2000, 2002, 2003, 2009 by Holman Bible Publishers. Used by permission. HCSB® is a federally registered trademark of Holman Bible Publishers.

Scripture quotations marked (AMP) are from the Amplified Bible, Copyright© 1954, 1958, 1962, 1964,1965, 1987 by The Lockman Foundation. Used by permission.

Scripture quotations marked (ISV) are from the Holy Bible: International Standard Version®. Copyright© 1996-forever by The ISV Foundation. ALL RIGHTS RESERVED INTERNATIONALLY. Used by permission.

DEVOTIONAL COLORING JOURNAL

VOLUME II

From Why To I

Ponder the path of your feet; then all your ways will be sure. Proverbs 4:26 ESV

If we want Jesus' heart, we must be present and see the broken world around us. When we ponder the pain we witness, our hearts will break. The power of pondering happens when we use our questions about injustice and pain to transform our questions from, "Why did this happen?" to "How can I help?" When we transform our "why" to "I," we see that although the world is filled with "why", "I" have the power to be a light in the darkness. ~ *Beth Mabe Gianopulos*

Jesus, Help us slow down and see the world we live in. Open our eyes to the things that break Your heart. When we wonder why so much pain and sadness can be in the world, guide us and show us how we can bring some light and hope to the darkness. Thank You for loving us. In Jesus' name, Amen. ~ Beth Mabe Gianopulos

Boasting in the Lord

But it is from Him that you are in Christ Jesus, who became God-given wisdom for us—our righteousness, sanctification, and redemption, in order that, as it is written: The one who boasts must boast in the Lord. 1 Corinthians 1:30-31 HCSB

Our society places a huge amount of significance in our success. But God's standards are different. You don't need to have your name in lights to accomplish His will; you simply need to follow in the steps of Christ. All that we are and all that we have is through Jesus. If we are going to boast, let's boast about a God who loves us deeply and redeemed us through the blood of Jesus. *~ Annah Matthews*

God, Give me eyes to see as You see. Give me ears to hear what You hear. Give me a heart that feels what You feel. Holy Spirit, show me how to do what Jesus would do. In Jesus' name, Amen. ~ Beth Mabe Gianopulos

Valuable

But now, O Lord, thou art our Father; we are the clay, and thou our potter; and we all are the work of thy hand. Isaiah 64:8 KJV

Several years ago my sister agreed to trade one family heirloom for another. She got a treasured breakfast nook bench from me that my grandfather built; I got the wood and plaster frame she had that was no less valuable. It has been hanging in my bedroom sans painting and with the worn lamp cord exposed that my father used for hanging it. I was delighted to cherish and display the tattered frame just as it was. Recently, the frame came down for renovations. When it was time to go back to its chosen place, I just couldn't leave it the way it was. With the frame in my lap, I lovingly added clay to the holes in the broken plaster. It went back on display refurbished, renewed, and whole once again. When we become broken and worn, God cherishes us nonetheless. Just like my treasured frame, He carefully refurbishes us, renews us and refines us in His beautiful and perfect way. ~ *Betty 'B' Shoopman*

Lord, I know You tell me that I am a treasure, but some days I simply feel broken. Remind me today that You specialize in broken made beautiful. Help me to hold onto that truth and live as the valuable child You say that I am. In Jesus' name, Amen. ~ Luann Prater

ENCOURAGEMENT CAFÉ DEVOTIONAL COLORING JOURNAL

Walk This Way

...and whenever you turn to the right or to the left, your ears will hear this command behind you: 'This is the way. Walk in it.' Isaiah 30:21 HCSB

The question is often asked, "How do I know the will of God?" Be still, lean in, and learn to hear and listen to the voice of the Lord. Through reading the Word of God, we learn to discern between our self-talk and the voice of our Father. Receiving Godly counsel from trusted friends and talking to God through prayer are ways to distinguish the Spirit of the Lord. Ask the Lord to help you listen to His voice so that you know when He speaks, you walk in His ways. ~ *Annah Matthews*

Jesus, Here I am again, hiding in the dark. Instead of shining, I've retreated into the shadows. Will You remind me that You are all I need to shine? I don't have to be like anyone else, You have created me to be perfectly unique, and that is enough. Thank You for allowing the light to shine through this cracked vessel, in Jesus' name, Amen.
~ Luann Prater

ENCOURAGEMENT CAFÉ DEVOTIONAL COLORING JOURNAL

Mirror, Mirror on the Wall

You are altogether beautiful, my darling, and there is no blemish in you.
Song of Solomon 4:7 NASB

Curiously, when looking in the mirror this morning, instead of noticing the insecure woman I had grown into, I saw myself through God's eyes. I saw His overwhelming love empowering me to live a life of spiritual abundance, security, and confidence. When you look into the mirror, what do you see? Do you look beyond your reflection to see yourself as God's beloved, treasured, and adored daughter? I challenge you to see yourself for who you are... altogether beautiful. ~ *Zoe Elmore*

Good morning Jesus, I pray that You would bless and keep me today. Make Your face to shine upon me and be gracious to me. I ask that You fill me with Your grace and love so that wherever I go, my actions will bring You glory. I pray Lord for You to turn Your face toward me and give me peace, In the name that is above every name, Jesus, Amen.
~ Zoe Elmore

ENCOURAGEMENT CAFÉ DEVOTIONAL COLORING JOURNAL

Becoming More Than I Am

***But if you're content to be simply yourself, you will become more than yourself.
Luke 14:11b MSG***

Somewhere along the way, I bought into the lie that looking and acting like the world would satisfy the emptiness within me. Because I am always striving to be someone else, I am not content with who I am. If I am discontent with who I am, I will never find the unique path that God has planned just for me. However, if I am content to be myself, God promises that I will become more than myself. ~ *Beth Mabe Gianopulos*

Jesus, You know our hearts. You know that we sometimes look to the wrong things to bring contentment and happiness. Help us to be content to be ourselves. Show us that by being content to simply be who we are, You will make us more than we ever dreamed we could be. In Jesus' name, Amen. ~ Beth Mabe Gianopulos

The Gift of Grace

For it is by grace you have been saved, through faith — and this is not from yourselves, it is the gift of God — not by works, so that no one can boast.
Ephesians 2:8-9 NIV

Grace is the gift of God. Through the precious blood of Jesus, God extends His grace to each of us regardless of our ethnicity or background. When we turn back to Him in faith, we accept the gift of His grace, and He saves us as His own for eternity. Nothing can separate us from His everlasting love because nothing can separate us from Him!
~ *Mindy Lee Hopman*

Heavenly Father, I praise You for the gift of grace that came at the expense of Your precious Son. Thank You for the lavish love You extended to me. My heart is full and I am eternally grateful. In the precious name of Jesus I pray, Amen. ~ Mindy Lee Hopman

ENCOURAGEMENT CAFÉ DEVOTIONAL COLORING JOURNAL

A Shining Light

In the same way, let your light shine before others, so that they may see your good works and give glory to your Father who is in heaven. Matthew 5:16 ESV

A ship in a dark sea only needs a small beacon of light from miles away to know which direction to navigate. A lighthouse points a ship in the right direction. In a world that is dark and always searching for the light, you can be that beacon of hope. Let the light of Christ shine out through you and let it point others to His good works in you.
~ Annah Matthews

O Lord, How amazing are Your ways! You dwell in us and it is more than we can fathom. When we spend time with You we can't help but shine! Today help me to boldly walk into this dark world with the Light of Christ, in Jesus' name, Amen. ~ Luann Prater

Deeper Still

...having been firmly rooted and now being built up in Him and established in your faith, just as you were instructed, and overflowing with gratitude.
Colossians 2:7 NASB

Firmly established roots thrive, gain strength, and overflow with gratitude from the gifts of God's goodness. May your roots grow deep into Him as your heart grows in the understanding of His immense love for you. Beloved, you are adored by the King of kings! When your roots grow deep into Him, you can't help but bloom right where you are planted! ~ *Mindy Lee Hopman*

Heavenly Father, I praise You for the faith family tree in which I am grafted the moment I believe. I praise You for the deep roots in You that establish who I am so that I may not only survive, but thrive. My heart overflows with gratitude. In the precious name of Jesus, Amen. ~ Mindy Lee Hopman

Baby Steps

Whoever is faithful in very little is also faithful in much,
and whoever is unrighteous in very little is also unrighteous in much.
Luke 16:10 HCSB

We want to make a huge impact and leave a legacy, but we often wonder how we'll ever get there. Jesus is clear in this passage that He entrusts the small things to us to grow our faith into even bigger things. We wonder when the next big break will occur or when we'll be noticed, but we often miss the very things right in front of our eyes. The ministry in our home, to our neighbors, or serving behind the scenes are the exact places where God teaches and refines our faith. What ministry is right before you that He is using to develop your story of faith? ~ *Annah Matthews*

Lord, It is easy for us to think we are off Your radar. It can be hard to comprehend You really know our hearts' desire. Delving into Your Word clearly teaches us how to rely on You to direct our lives. When we stay close to You, Lord, You guide our small steps of faith. Following Your direction grows our testimony of Your great love. Thank You Jesus, Amen.
~ Betty "B" Shoopman

Be the Example

Let no one despise your youth; instead, you should be an example to the believers in speech, in conduct, in love, in faith, in purity. 1 Timothy 4:12 HCSB

There is no age bracket of ministry to the Lord. He equips each one of us in every season of life to prepare us and bring forth fruit. As youth, we have a circle of influence among friends and peers that others don't have. As newlyweds, we have the ministry of marriage among those around us. As mothers, our home is a training ground for the next generation. As single women, we can devote more time to praying, serving, teaching, and traveling. As retirees, we have the honor to look back on God's faithfulness and encourage those behind us to press on. Let no one despise any age; you are always in ministry and an example to others. ~ *Annah Matthews*

Lord, Make me ready. You know me and my tendency to shrink back and think others will do a better job, or have more talent, or shine brighter, yet You have called each of us to take steps of obedience. Ready my feet, sustain my walk and pour through me with all the confidence I need to go where You lead, in Jesus' name, Amen. ~ Luann Prater

ENCOURAGEMENT CAFÉ DEVOTIONAL COLORING JOURNAL

Rejoice in the Lord

Rejoice in the Lord always. I will say it again: Rejoice! Let your graciousness be known to everyone. The Lord is near. Philippians 4:4-5 HCSB

How can I be known as one who lives a life of joy and graciousness? Choose to rejoice in the Lord. Live a life that abundantly speaks love, joy, and graciousness towards others. When we have Christ living in our hearts, we have a different kind of joy, and we should look different than others. Share the joy of Christ with those around you and be gracious in telling others about the goodness of God. The Lord is near to you. Rejoice! ~ *Annah Matthews*

Holy Spirit, You are welcome here. In every life, in every heart, we pray in agreement for You to flood our hearts. May Your presence help us live the lives You have set before us. Stretch us Lord. Join us together in one accord. We are Yours and You are our God. Thank You for comradery in You. We rejoice in You, Lord, Amen. ~ Betty 'B' Shoopman

A Clear Conscience

I always do my best to have a clear conscience toward God and men.
Acts 24:16 HCSB

Allowing God to transform our hearts and minds can be a difficult process when God calls things to our minds that we need to confess. However, having a clear conscience before God and men doesn't mean we live in shame and regret. Instead, we live in freedom by confessing our sins to Him and moving forward. Claim His steadfast love for you and walk in the freedom of being forgiven with a clear conscience.
~ *Annah Matthews*

Lord, Thank You for teaching us what forgiveness and love look like! We can get so bogged down in guilt and shame and unforgiveness until Your Word reveals the cure. Jesus, You are the perfect example of unconditional love. Show me today how I can love lavishly. Your forgiveness was complete. Teach me today to extend that not only to others but to myself as well. In Jesus' name, Amen. ~ Luann Prater

ENCOURAGEMENT CAFÉ DEVOTIONAL COLORING JOURNAL

Walk by Faith

For we live by faith, not by sight. II Corinthians 5:7 NIV

Our finite eyes cannot comprehend what our Father's infinite eyes can see. When we place our faith in Him, He lives in us. And just as Jesus overcame death, so will we, because we are One in Him. So we give thanks to God for being our Living Hope and for working behind the scenes fighting battles we cannot see. Beloved, faith is not a feeling. Faith is trusting God even when we cannot see. ~ *Mindy Lee Hopman*

Lord Jesus, You are the Alpha and Omega, the Beginning and the End. We know that full well, and yet we stumble over our current circumstances as if they are unique and unbearable. You are the Mighty Conqueror, the One who fights our battles and comes to our rescue. You are not surprised by anything. I surrender my striving into Your sanctifying hands. In Jesus' name, Amen. ~ Luann Prater

ENCOURAGEMENT CAFÉ DEVOTIONAL COLORING JOURNAL

Strength For Our Journeys

Consider it all joy, my brethren, when you encounter various trials, knowing that the testing of your faith produces endurance. James 1:2-3 NASB

Sisters, life can be tough. Divorce, unemployment, and sickness are but a few trials that many of us face. James does not say that we *may* encounter trials; we *will* experience them. But there is good news! When our faith is tested, we receive strength. No matter what we endure, Jesus promised to be with us every step of the way. He fills us with strength and faith for our journey. ~ *Lara Sadowski*

Jesus, Thank You for Your promises. Thank You for taking the impossible trials that we face and using them for our good. While we are in the heartache, remind us of Your promises and renew our hope. In Jesus' name, Amen. ~ Beth Mabe Gianopulos

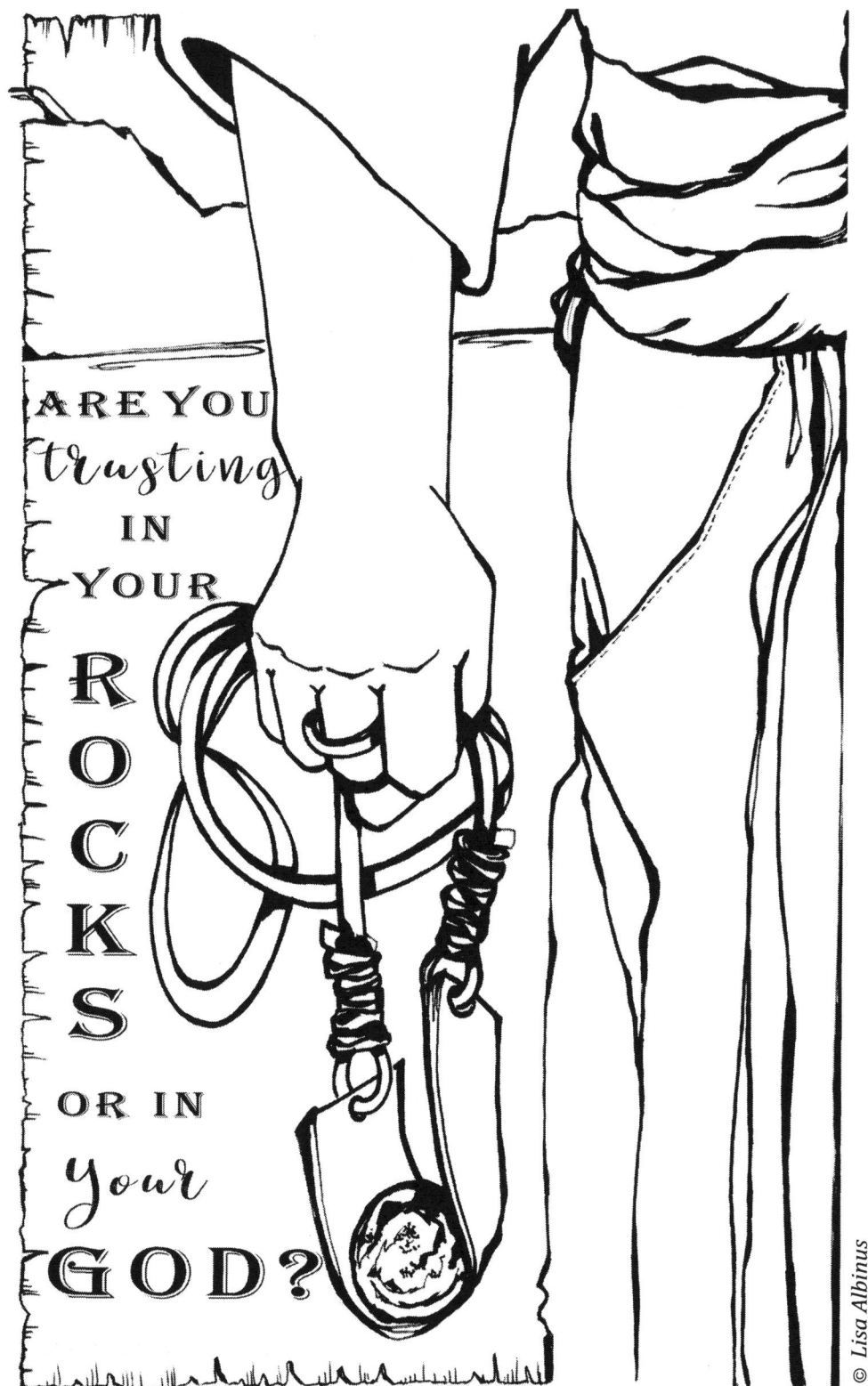

ENCOURAGEMENT CAFÉ DEVOTIONAL COLORING JOURNAL

Rocky Places

...for the battle is the Lord's and He will give you into our hands.
1 Samuel 17:47b NASB

We may be facing a "giant" today that the world tells us cannot be defeated. We may have put all of our strength into the rocks we have gathered to defend ourselves. With eyes focused on our giant, the battle, and our rocks, we lose the larger picture of the One who surrounds us. What if we entered into our circumstances in the name of the Lord of hosts? What if we put our rocks down and trusted in the God of angel armies? We are promised through Scripture that the battle is the Lord's and that He goes before us. Victory is found within Him, never in our rocks. *~ Lisa Albinus*

Father, I am such a control freak. Forgive me for trying to take over when You are the One in charge. I don't need to have all the answers or know the way today, I only need to trust in You. Help me with my flimsy faith. Teach me to lean into You as You fight my battle. In Jesus' name, Amen. ~ Luann Prater

ENCOURAGEMENT CAFÉ DEVOTIONAL COLORING JOURNAL

What's Keeping You Up At Night?

***I reflect at night on who you are, O Lord; therefore, I obey your instructions.
Psalm 119:55 NLT***

While my family sleeps peacefully, my thoughts race from one subject to another. Anxiety invades each thought, shattering any hope of sleep. I've learned to stop this downward spiral by reflecting on God's character. When I choose to name one godly character trait for every letter of the alphabet I'm able to sleep peacefully, awakening with a quiet and confident spirit. If nights are filled with anxiety, focus on the character of God. It changes everything. ~ *Zoe Elmore*

Heavenly Father, Although I don't know what Your plans are for me today, I awaken with confidence knowing You know Your plans for my life. Your plans are to prosper me, to give me hope and a future. I'm grateful for Your unconditional love that reminds me that Your mercies are new every morning and You hold my today and my future in Your hands. In the name that is above every name, Jesus, Amen. ~ Zoe Elmore

God told Abram: Leave your country, your family, and your father's home for a land I will show you.

Genesis 12:1 MSG

© Lisa Albinus

ENCOURAGEMENT CAFÉ DEVOTIONAL COLORING JOURNAL

Everlasting Love

...and hope does not disappoint, because the love of God has been poured out within our hearts through the Holy Spirit who was given to us. Romans 5:5 NASB

My capacity to love is limited in my strength. That is why I must rely on His love to help me navigate through life. When I rely on my strength alone, I can run out of the ability to care for more than a few people in my inner circle. If I'm completely transparent, at times, I feel incapable of truly caring for and loving even these few. They may not realize I'm depleted, but deep within I know I am. It is as if my love reservoir begins to dry up to the point of desert-like conditions in my soul. Weariness and feelings of insignificance creep in, hoping to attach somewhere in a destructive and permanent way. Then the Father reminds me...FAITH TRIUMPHS! His love for me is everlasting because I believe He is who He declares Himself to be through His Word.
~ *Debra Winningham*

Real love is so hard for us to comprehend Lord. Our world tells us love is conditional, yet before we were born, You sent Your Son so that I could experience Your Everlasting Love. Thank You for demonstrating that kind of love. May Your Spirit pour that love through me and onto others today. In Jesus' name, Amen. ~ Luann Prater

FOR I, THE LORD THY GOD, WILL HOLD THY RIGHT HAND SAYING UNTO THEE,

Fear Not:
I WILL HELP THEE.

ISAIAH 41:13 KJV

© Lisa Albinus

Be a Burden Carrier

Carry each other's burdens, and in this way you will fulfill the law of Christ.
Galatians 6:2 NIV

When the Lord healed a boy in our town by taking him home to heaven, I wept for a family I didn't know and for a child who wasn't mine. With Holy Spirit gentleness God said, "This is what Galatians 6:2 looks like." Then the vision came. The farmhouse where they lived had a black cloud over it. Whenever someone grieved, a piece of the cloud drifted away. They were still hurting and their son was still gone, but some suffering was alleviated because of the fulfilling of how Scripture prayer works. We are His, and He is real. ~ *Dawn Mast*

Jesus, Thank You for the blessings You have poured upon us. Open our eyes and our hearts to all that we have to be thankful for. Give us strength to continue to thank You, even as our hearts are breaking. Bring healing to us as we thank You and praise Your name. In Jesus' name, Amen. ~ Beth Mabe Gianopulos

You thought you buried me.

But you only helped me BLOOM.

© Hannah-Rose Albinus

ENCOURAGEMENT CAFÉ DEVOTIONAL COLORING JOURNAL

Gracious Words

Let your speech always be gracious, seasoned with salt, so that you may know how you ought to answer each person. Colossians 4:6 ESV

Sometimes every ounce of your body wants to lash out in anger. You get that small, quiet gut-check in your spirit to stop, listen, and think. The consequences of the next word, which is about to fall out of your mouth, can bring life or bring death. As the cliché goes, "You can't unring a bell." Ask the Holy Spirit into the moments of high emotions to give you holy restraint and check yourself. Ask Him to allow your words to be gracious and seasoned with the salt of Christ-likeness. You are far more likely to be heard if you allow the Holy Spirit to lead your speech and to guide you with His answer. ~ *Annah Matthews*

Jesus, Thank You for family and friends. Even when our family and friends hurt us or drive us crazy, help us to look for the good in them. Remind us that love looks for the best in others, and help us to continue to look for the good until we find it. In Jesus' name, Amen. ~ Beth Mabe Gianopulos

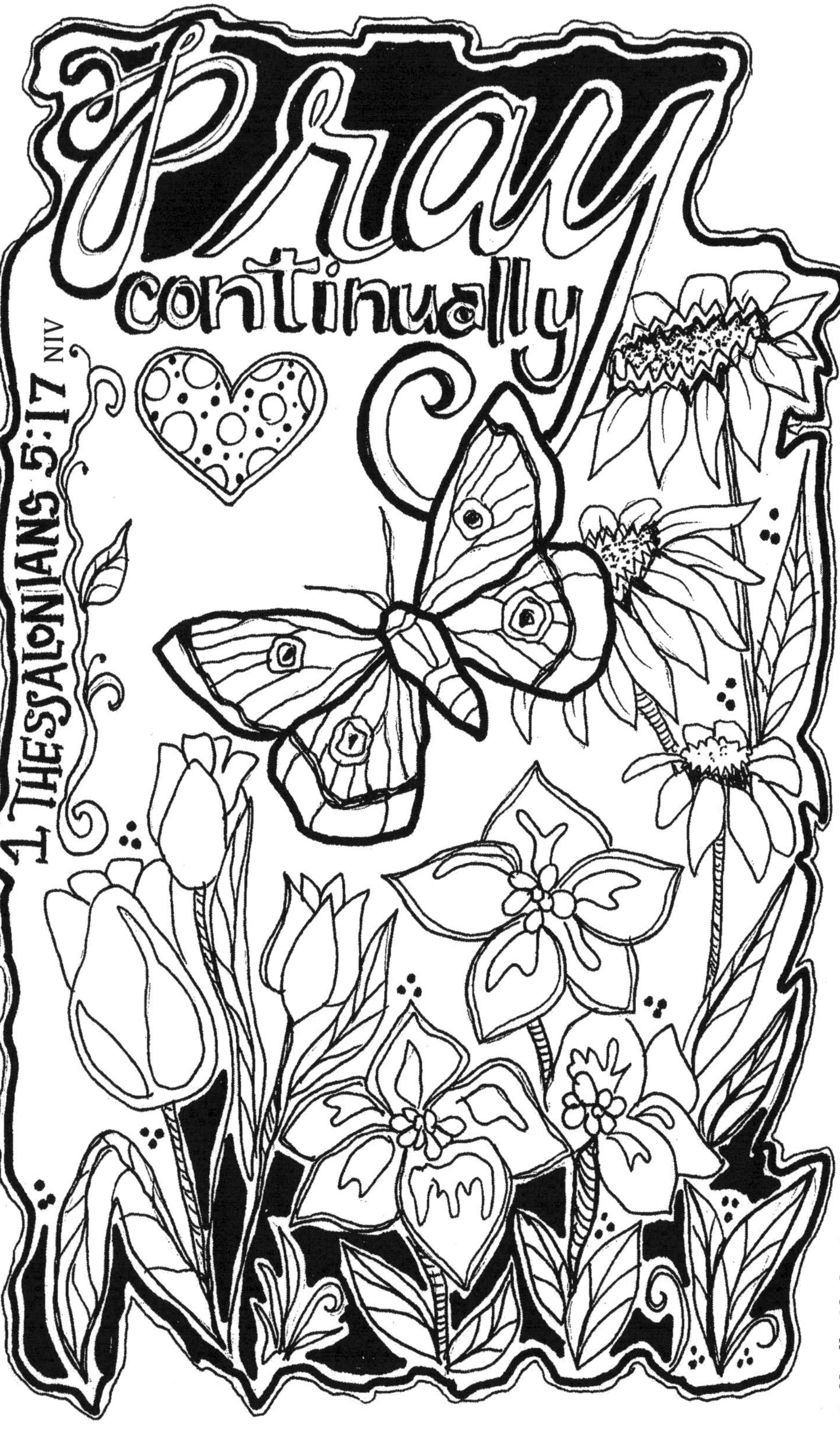

Pray
continually
1 THESSALONIANS 5:17 NIV

Demonstrate

Rejoice always, pray continually, give thanks in all circumstances; for this is God's will for you in Christ Jesus. 1 Thessalonians 5:16-18 NIV

How do we give God "radical" thanks while in the midst of suffering? The night Jesus was betrayed He gave thanks. He broke bread and drank wine, saying, "Do this in remembrance of Me." Since Jesus himself suffered, and His suffering is the ultimate healer of ours, maybe through his demonstration of thanks, we can offer the same measure in return? He's been there. He's walked the Golgotha road. Can you give radical thanks in your suffering, too? ~ *Jessica Maples*

Father, You've shown us Your Will for our lives. To be joyful, pray continually and to give thanks in all circumstances sounds impossible and yet, You've given us the way, through Your Son. Today, I choose to follow Your Will. In Jesus' name, Amen. ~ Luann Prater

BUT IN ALL THESE THINGS WE *overwhelmingly* CONQUER *through Him who loved us.*

Romans 8:37
NASB

© Betty 'B' Shoopman

Cleaned Up

I can do all things [which He has called me to do] through Him who strengthens and empowers me [to fulfill His purpose—I am self-sufficient in Christ's sufficiency; I am ready for anything and equal to anything through Him who infuses me with inner strength and confident peace.] AMP

There it went. The whole mop bucket of dirty water spilled all over my clean floor. I thought I was done cleaning and the realization came that it was going to take more time and effort to clean up this mess. There were no shortcuts. I want shortcuts sometimes, but God knows exactly what I need. Sometimes it is essential we put more effort into what we are doing. Time is not as important as is the task at hand. Are we ready to endure what it takes to follow Him? He will always come to our aid if we let Him. He loves to clean up messes. Oh, the rewards are great when we let Him lead.
~ *Betty 'B' Shoopman*

Father, I lift my friend to You. Help her to let go of the need to fix everything. Lead her to rest in Your presence. Give her unexpected moments of calm and restorative blankets of Peace. Help my friend target the thoughts that overwhelm her and replace them with Your truth. Hold her I pray, so tightly that she feels the warmth of Your embrace. In Jesus' name, Amen. ~ Luann Prater

© Lisa Albinus

ENCOURAGEMENT CAFÉ DEVOTIONAL COLORING JOURNAL

Dare to Believe

Those who sow with tears will reap with songs of joy. Psalm 126:5 NIV

What a precious promise from God! Have you been in a place where you are familiar with tears that come often? Have you walked through loneliness, grief, or depression? You are not alone. Many of us have been at that place of weeping. With God, there is always hope, friend, even during a time of struggle! Have you ever considered that the tears are a gift? They are a release of all that is inside, and a precious promise from God, that joy will come. His Word says, "Weeping may endure for the night, but joy comes in the morning." How? Well, His promise says, "Those that sow in tears will reap in joy." Could you dare today to think of your tears as little seeds of joy? That though the tears fall, they are seeds of the joy that God will restore in your life. Could you dare to believe He is big enough to bring you a harvest of joy? You are never without hope, never alone, and never without seeds for greater joy in your life! What a gift. ~ *Theresa Mills*

Lord, We often get bogged down in life and forget that You have given us every tool we need to overcome. Your Word tells us to rejoice always, and we tend to question, how? Yet the next two words tell us how to rejoice. To rejoice, we have to pray continually! Remind us of those two words when life feels less than joyful. Today, I CHOOSE to thank You. My circumstances change, yet You never do. That is the reason to pray and praise You. In Jesus' name I pray, Amen. ~ Luann Prater

FOR THE SPIRIT GOD GAVE US
DOES NOT MAKE US
TIMID,
BUT GIVES US POWER, and LOVE & SELF-DISCIPLINE.
We Can Do It!
2 TIMOTHY 1:7
NIV

I Will Follow You

He guides me in the paths of righteousness for His name's sake.
Psalm 23:3b NASB

God can see the "big picture" from the beginning to the end, while we can only see a "snapshot" of time. He has graciously equipped you with certain gifts and skills to use right where you are, and He knows where you fit into the "big picture." It's natural for us to want to go our way, but He wants us to trust Him and follow Him. The good Shepherd has already gone ahead, cleared the way, and made the rough places smooth. On the path He has created for you, you will thrive! It's up to us to choose to follow Him with grateful hearts for what He has already done, and what He continues to do in our lives. ~ *Mindy Lee Hopman*

_____
_____
_____
_____
_____
_____
_____
_____
_____
_____
_____
_____
_____
_____
_____
_____
_____
_____
_____
_____
_____
_____
_____
_____

Father, Thank You for seeing value in us at any age. We choose each day to be used for Your glory. Today give me the confidence to rise up and go where You lead. In Jesus' name, Amen. ~ Luann Prater

...WE HAVE THIS TREASURE IN JARS OF CLAY TO SHOW THAT THIS ALL-SURPASSING *power is from God and not from us.* II Corinthians 4:7

NIV

© Betty 'B' Shoopman

Overflowing

May the God of hope fill you with all joy and peace as you trust in him, so that you may overflow with hope by the power of the Holy Spirit. Romans 15:13 NIV

Isn't it just like God go above and beyond? He doesn't only offer us hope, although that is so powerful. He wants to fill us with all joy and peace as we trust in Him! Think about that. Filled with joy - and the joy of the Lord is our strength - therefore filled with strength! Now, if that weren't enough, He wants to fill us with peace! Many times in the Bible you will see the phrase, "Peace be unto you." It was a spoken blessing over the hearer that meant, "May your life be filled with health, prosperity and victory!" The God of hope fills us with joy and peace as we trust in Him. Hope is the earnest expectation that our good God has something good in store for you. I love the acronyms for H.O.P.E. - Hold On Patiently Expecting! or Hold On Praising Expectantly! You just know God has something good on the way. God doesn't want you to just have hope, He wants you to overflow with hope by the power of His spirit! What happens when something overflows? It gets everywhere!! So the hope of God overflowing out of your life can't help but impact everything around you. So today, thank God for filling you with all joy and peace, as you trust in Him, so that you will overflow with hope by the power of His spirit! ~ *Theresa Mills*

Father, You are our hope! Help us to fully trust in You so that the joy and peace we long for in our everyday life will not only fill us but overflow onto others. You've placed people in our paths so that they might see how a hope-filled life looks. May Your power flow through us today we pray. In Jesus' name, Amen. ~ Luann Prater

Warfare Worship

© Lisa Albinus

Today We Worship

Worship the LORD with gladness; come before him with joyful songs.
Psalm 100:2 NIV

One of the toughest times in my life was when there was extreme tension in my home. Some days it was hard to imagine life without struggle. In the midst of a dark day, a song pressed through to the forefront of my mind that I once sang in church. At first, I struggled to mumble the words, but as I allowed them to fall from my lips, I recalled every word. The song began to flow freely from my heart as if angels were marching the lyrics from my soul into victory. The Bible tells us that God inhabits the praises of His people. Sing! And be filled with joy! ~ *Luann Prater*

Lord God, You are worthy to be praised. Forgive me for being too overwhelmed to sing. Restore gladness to my heart through music and singing. May every word that flows be offered back to You in praise! In Jesus' name, I pray, Amen. ~ Luann Prater

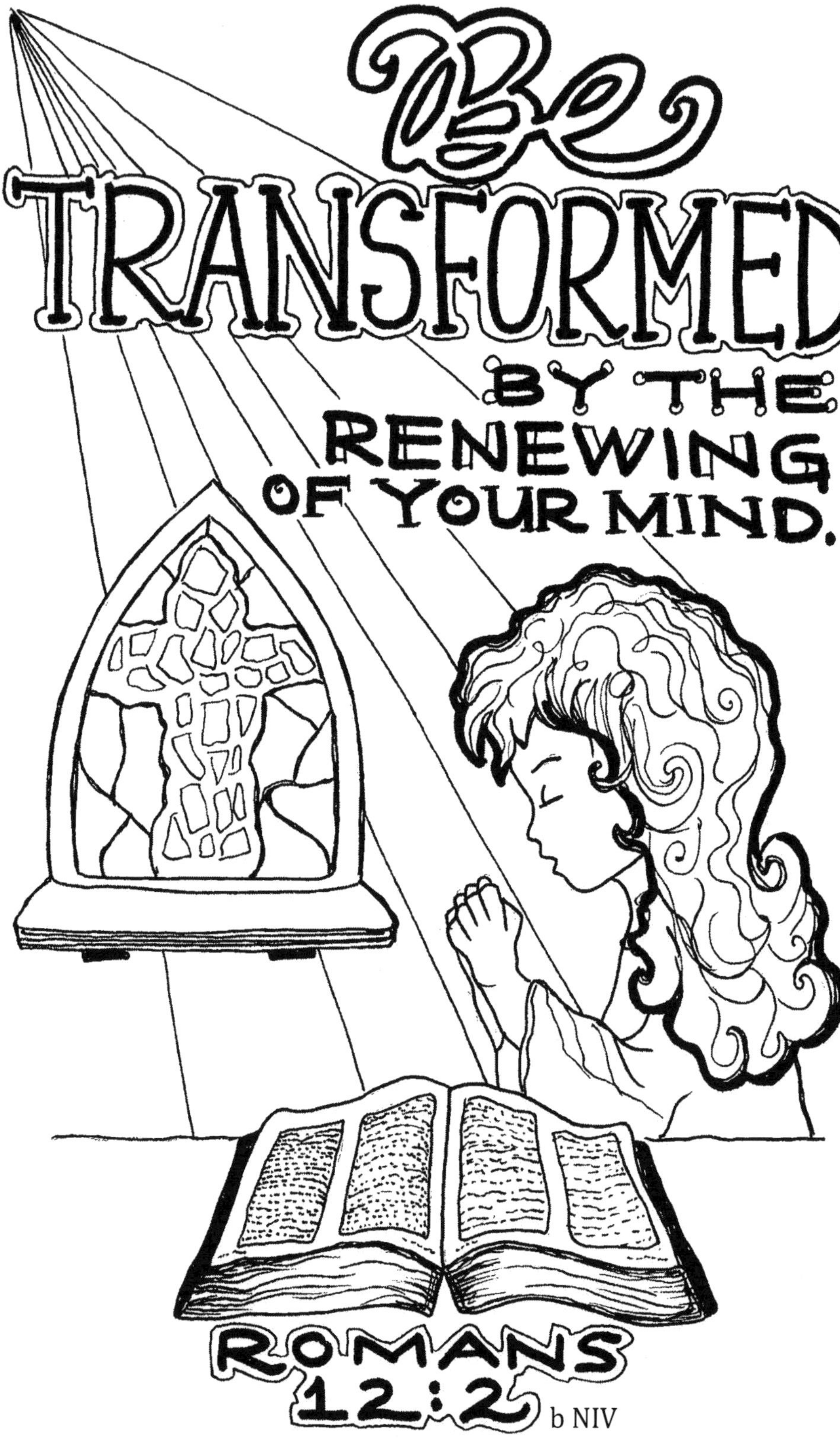

b NIV

ENCOURAGEMENT CAFÉ DEVOTIONAL COLORING JOURNAL

Mind Grip

Your word is a lamp for my feet, a light on my path. Psalm 119:105 NIV

Renewing our mind takes two things, intentional effort and regular commitment to God. When we genuinely seek a closer walk with the Lord, Satan will pull out all the stops. His greatest hope is to stop us from doing God's will. What struggle gripped you this week? Let's commit to spending more time in God's Word this week and to intentionally stop doing the things that once caused us to sin. ~ *Luann Prater*

_____
_____
_____
_____
_____
_____
_____
_____
_____
_____
_____
_____
_____
_____
_____
_____
_____
_____
_____
_____
_____
_____
_____
_____
_____

Abba Father, I fall before You knowing that I messed up again, and yet You promise that Your mercies are new every day. Will You pour Your mercy on me right now and empower me to make intentional decisions that will keep me away from temptation? Renew my mind as Your Word washes over me with truth. I pray in Jesus' name, Amen.
~ Luann Prater

THE ETERNAL GOD IS YOUR REFUGE

and underneath are *everlasting arms.*
Duet. 33:27a NIV

© Betty 'B' Shoopman

Hide Me

You are my hiding place;
you will protect me from trouble and surround me with songs of deliverance.
Psalm 32:7 NIV

Sometimes I like to hide. I hide maybe under my blankets, maybe on the couch, or maybe behind a piece of chocolate. When life gets strained, I often want to check out. In those moments, God reminds me that I'm not in this alone. This passage makes me think of a hero who pulls me from danger and tucks me into a hiding place and throws himself around me as a shield. Isn't it so reassuring that God promises to be our hero, our refuge, our shield within His arms? Rest there today. ~ *Luann Prater*

_____
_____
_____
_____
_____
_____
_____
_____
_____
_____
_____
_____
_____
_____
_____
_____
_____
_____
_____
_____
_____
_____

O Lord, I'm tired. I long for rest yet find more on my to-do list than I'm capable of handling. Instead of chocolate, or comfort from anything second-rate, I'm rushing to the shelter of Your arms. Hold me today and allow me to find the much-needed rest my body requires. I pray in Jesus' name, Amen. ~ Luann Prater

Because HE BENDS DOWN to listen, I WILL PRAY as long AS I HAVE breath.

Psalm 116:2
NLT

© Lisa Albinus

He is Listening

Call to me and I will answer you and tell you great and unsearchable things you do not know. Jeremiah 33:3 NIV

She bounced into the living room after a full day at school, then play practice. She counted on me being awake and ready to listen. We snuggled into a heap on the couch, and my teenage daughter told me everything about her day. Oh, how I cherish those memories. There are days when I curl up in a heap and lean into my Father's arms, knowing He bends down to listen to the events of my day. You are deeply loved. Curl up and talk to Him today. ~ *Luann Prater*

___

Lord, I lift my friend to You today and ask for divine discernment and Your wisdom to invade her mind. Wash over her with the assurance that You've gone before her and the path is clear. Help her to see it as she walks it in faith. Hold her and carry her when she gets weak. Will You allow her to literally feel Your arms wrap around her? We trust You Father. We know You love deeply and care about every decision we make. Pour in and through my friend today. In Jesus' name, Amen. ~ Luann Prater

He makes me lie down in green pastures,

HE LEADS ME BESIDE QUIET WATERS,

HE REFRESHES MY SOUL.

Psalm 23:22,23a
NIV

© Betty 'B' Shoopman

You Are More

Consider how the wild flowers grow. They do not labor or spin. Yet I tell you, not even Solomon in all his splendor was dressed like one of these. Luke 12:27 NIV

Have you ever felt 'less than'? If we're honest, there are times in our lives when we compare ourselves to those around us. We feel as though we are not thin enough, smart enough, or rich enough to fit in. It's easy to spot the obvious portrait of pride, those who look down at others while climbing up on a pedestal; but can we recognize the extreme opposite of pride? When we feel inadequate, insecure, and full of guilt we are saying to God, "Your Holy Spirit is not enough." Today, inhabit your worth, for you are priceless just the way you are. ~ *Luann Prater*

Father, Forgive me for longing to be a lily when You've created me to be a daisy. Remind me that every flower in Your garden has beauty and purpose. Teach me to live this day as Your splendid creation! In Jesus' name, I pray, Amen. ~ Luann Prater